Q

WILD WICKED WONDERFUL

TOP 10:

BODY PARTS

By Virginia Loh-Hagan

45th Parallel Press

Published in the United States of America by Cherry Lake Publishing
Ann Arbor, Michigan
www.cherrylakepublishing.com

Content Adviser: Stephen Ditchkoff, Professor of Wildlife Ecology and Management, Auburn University, Alabama
Reading Adviser: Marla Conn MS, Ed., Literacy specialist, Read-Ability, Inc.
Book Designer: Melinda Millward

Photo Credits: © Attila JANDI/Shutterstock.com, cover, 1, 30; © Oleg Znamenskiy/Shutterstock.com, 5; © Davidov Oleh/Shutterstock.com, 6; © Zhiltsov Alexandr/Shutterstock.com, 6; © hagit berkovich/Shutterstock.com, 6, 7; © Klaus / http://www.flickr.com/ CC BY-SA 2.0, 8; © worldswildlifewonders/Shutterstock.com, 8; © Nature Picture Library / Alamy Stock Photo, 9; © ShotByRob/iStockphoto, 10; © Vladimir Wrangel/Shutterstock.com, 12; © SvetlanaSF/Shutterstock.com, 12; © JPL Designs/Shutterstock.com, 12, 14; © arrowsg/iStockphoto, 13; © javarman/Shutterstock.com, 16; © dennisvdw/iStockphoto, 16; © blickwinkel / Alamy Stock Photo, 17; © Utopia_88/Shutterstock.com, 18; © Utopianepal/Dreamstime.com, 18; © Cooper5022/Dreamstime.com, 18; © Hans Bentzen/Shutterstock.com, 19; © CarissaWWW/Thinkstock, 20; © duangnapa_b/Shutterstock.com, 20; © bushton3/iStockphoto, 20; © Nicholas Toh/Shutterstock.com, 21; © Afagundes/Dreamstime.com, 22; © Luciano Queiroz/Shutterstock.com, 22; © l i g h t p o e t/Shutterstock.com, 22; © Karelgallas/Dreamstime.com, 23; © PA Images / Alamy Stock Photo, 24; © Handout / Handout / Getty Images, 25; © Carrie Vonderhaar/Ocean Futures Society / Getty Images, 26; © chakkrachai nicharat/Shutterstock.com, 27; © Donovan van Staden/Shutterstock.com, 28; © Willyam Bradberry/Shutterstock.com, 28; © john michael evan potter/Shutterstock.com, 28; © Peter Betts/Shutterstock.com, 29; © megscapturedtreasures/Shutterstock.com, 30; © Paulhenk/Dreamstime.com, 30; © Stacey Ann Alberts/Shutterstock.com, 31

Graphic Element Credits: ©tukkki/Shutterstock.com, back cover, front cover, multiple interior pages; ©paprika/Shutterstock.com, back cover, front cover, multiple interior pages; ©Silhouette Lover/Shutterstock.com, multiple interior pages

45th Parallel Press is an imprint of Cherry Lake Publishing.

Library of Congress Cataloging-in-Publication Data

Names: Loh-Hagan, Virginia, author.
Title: Top 10 : body parts / by Virginia Loh-Hagan.Description: Ann Arbor : Cherry Lake Publishing, 2017. |
    Series: Extreme animals/wild wicked wonderful |Includes bibliographical references and index.
Identifiers: LCCN 2016029718| ISBN 9781634721400 (hardcover) | ISBN 9781634722063 (pdf) |
    ISBN 9781634722728 (pbk.) | ISBN 9781634723381 (ebook)
Subjects: LCSH: Animals–Juvenile literature. | Morphology (Animals)–Juvenile literature.
Classification: LCC QL49 .L8343 2017 | DDC 590–dc23
LC record available at https://lccn.loc.gov/2016029718

Printed in the United States of America
Corporate Graphics

About the Author

Dr. Virginia Loh-Hagan is an author, university professor, former classroom teacher, and curriculum designer. She has weird body parts. She has child-sized hands and can wear kid shoes. She lives in San Diego with her very tall husband and very naughty dogs. To learn more about her, visit www.virginialoh.com.

TABLE OF CONTENTS

INTRODUCTION

Animals move. They hunt. They touch. They sense. They feel. They use body parts to do these things. They have arms. They have legs. They have ears. They have eyes.

Body parts serve a **function**. They have a specific job. They do things. They're designed for a special purpose. They help animals survive in their habitats.

Some animals have extreme body parts. Their body parts are stranger. Their body parts are stronger. Their body parts are smarter. These animals have the most exciting body parts in the animal world!

Appendages are parts of an animal, like arms, legs, and tails.

Chapter one

FENNEC FOXES

Fennec foxes are the world's smallest **canids**. Canids are dogs, wolves, and foxes. Fennec foxes are **nocturnal**. They hunt at night. They avoid the hot sun. They live in North African deserts. They're 8 inches (20 centimeters) tall. They have huge ears. Their ears are 6 inches (15 cm) long.

Their ears help them survive heat. Their ears cool them down. They carry heat away from their bodies.

Their ears also help them hunt. They pick up sounds. Sounds travel into their eardrums. They hear the tiniest movements. They hear animals moving underground.

A Fennec fox's ears are packed with blood vessels that are close to the skin.

Chapter two
PLATYPUSES

Platypuses live in rivers. They live in Australia. They have many strange body parts. They have a duck's **bill**. Bills are beaks. They have a mole's body. They have a beaver's tail. They have otter feet. They look odd. But they're built to hunt. They hunt underwater.

They swim. Their webbed feet paddle. Their tail steers. They close their eyes. They close their ears. Folds of skin cover their eyes and ears. This stops water from entering. Their nostrils seal close. Their body is made to be underwater.

Platypuses use their webbed feet as propellers and their tails as rudders.

Their bill is special. It has hundreds of **receptors**. Receptors are feelers. They pick up tiny movements. They feel their **prey**. Prey are animals hunted as food.

Most mammals don't have poison like platypuses do.

Platypuses are special **mammals**. Mammals have hair or fur. They give birth to live young. They feed milk to their young. They're warm-blooded. Platypuses are different. They also lay eggs. Females make milk. But they don't have nipples. They're missing these body parts.

Males have another special body part. They have sharp stingers. Stingers are on their heels. They're on their back feet. The stingers have poison.

DID YOU KNOW...?

- Human ears grow about 1/800th of an inch every year. If humans could live for 16,000 years, we could have ears like fennec foxes.

- The first platypus specimen was brought to England in 1798. Scientists thought it had been stitched together from different animal parts.

- Very few people have seen a living giant squid. What we know about them comes from dead giant squids that wash on shore.

- Male fiddler crabs spend twice as long eating as females. They have to eat with one arm.

- Anteaters store up poison from eating poison ants. Because of this, they have few predators. Their bodies aren't affected by poison. Baby anteaters haven't eaten enough poison yet. They're prey for predators. They hide on their moms' backs.

- Elephant skeletons don't show trunks. There are no trunk bones.

- Giraffe necks have seven bones. Humans also have seven neck bones. But giraffes' neck bones are bigger.

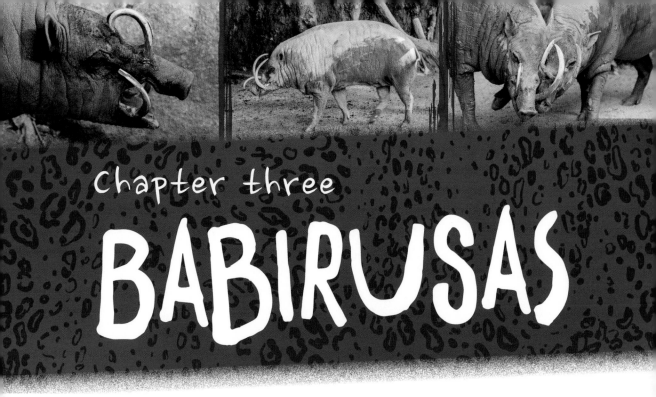

Chapter three

BABIRUSAS

Babirusas are called pig-deer. They have a pig's body. They have a pig's nose. They have deer legs. They have teeth that look like deer antlers. They live in Indonesia. They live in **tropical** forests. Tropical means hot and wet weather.

Males have special teeth. Their teeth are called **tusks**. Two tusks grow from their upper jaw. They grow straight. Then, they **rotate**, or turn. They go up through their mouth. They pierce through skin. They go through their nose. They keep growing. They curl backward. They curve toward their forehead.

Babirusas' tusks can grow to 17 inches (43 cm) long.

These tusks protect males' eyes during fights. The tusks act like shields.

To fight, males stand on their hind legs and jab their head upward.

Two more tusks grow out of their lower jaw. They grow upward. They're like knives. These tusks are weapons. They rub against the upper tusks. This helps keep them sharp. Males also rub their tusks against trees. This also sharpens their tusks.

They grind their tusks. They break tusks in fights. This is good. Otherwise tusks might pierce their skulls.

Females don't usually have upper tusks. Females use their bottom tusks to fight.

Babirusas fight for mates. They fight for space. They interlock tusks. They butt heads. They gore each other.

HUMANS DO WHAT?!?

Kayan women desire long necks. They live in Myanmar. They're known as "giraffe women." Women coil brass rings around their necks. The rings increase the distance between their ears and collarbones. The rings push down on the rib cage. The weight pushes down the muscles. This shortens the body. Necks look stretched out. Necks can get to be about 10 inches (25.4 cm) tall. It's dangerous when rings are removed. Neck muscles are weak. They can't support the head. Women start wearing rings at age 5. They add one ring per year until marriage. Some believe this tradition started to protect against tiger bites. Some think it's to make women look like dragons. Some think it's a way to honor culture and history. A Kayan woman said, "These neck coils mean a lot to me because I inherited them from my grandma."

Chapter four
AYE-AYES

Aye-ayes are **primates**. Primates include humans, apes, and monkeys. They're lemurs. They're nocturnal. They live in Madagascar.

They look odd. They're a collection of body parts. They have a **rodent**'s head. Rodents are animals like rats and mice. They have beaver teeth. They have bat ears. They have a fox's tail. They have a monkey's body.

They have witches' hands. They have bony middle fingers. Their middle fingers are skinny. They're long. They're three times longer than other fingers. They tap on wood. They

An aye-aye's middle finger is like a skewer. Skewers are skinny sticks that hold food together.

have big floppy ears. Their ears listen for sounds. They bite holes in the wood. They use their middle fingers to dig out bugs.

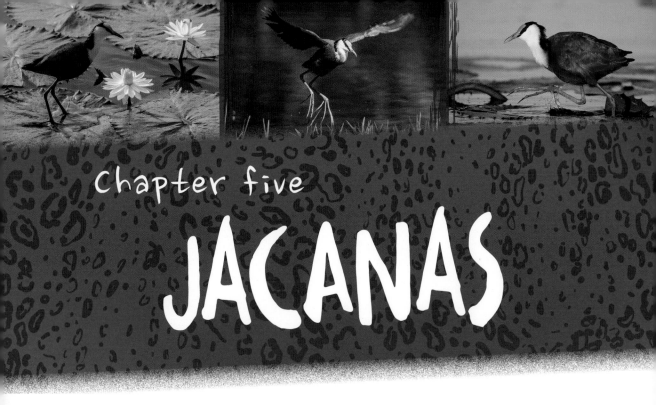

Chapter five
JACANAS

Jacanas are waterbirds. They live in the tropics. They live in South America. There's not much dry land. They walk on water plants. They swim. They dive.

They have long legs. They have long toes. They have the longest toes compared to body size of any birds. They have long claws. They use their toes to turn over leaves. This is how they find prey.

Their big feet let them walk on floating plants. They spread their weight. They do this over a large area. They run over floating plants.

Jacanas' feet are 60 percent of their body length.

Jacanas are called lily trotters. They spend most of their time near the water.

Chapter six

FiDDLER CRABS

Male fiddler crabs have one major claw. The major claw is much larger than the other claw.

Males wave their major claw. They attract females. Females like big claws. Big claws make bigger and better **burrows**. Burrows are underground homes. There's more space and heat for females to lay eggs. Females like when males wave more. Claws are heavy. Waving is hard work. Males show they're fit.

Males use their major claw to fight. They fight other males. They fight over females. They fight over space. Sometimes,

Different crab species have different claw colors.

males lose their major claw. Then they regrow a new one.
But they hide until the new claw hardens.

Chapter seven
ANTEATERS

Anteaters live in South America. They eat ants and termites. These bugs live in small hills.

Anteaters appear to have a long nose. But it's really a long jaw with a nose at the tip. They smell very well. They sniff the ground. They find ant hills. They have strong arms. They have strong claws. They rip open ant hills.

They have a long tongue. Their tongue is 2 feet (61 cm) long. It has **mucus** on it. Mucus is like snot. It makes tongues sticky. Anteaters use their tongue. They poke it into the hills. They do this 150 times a minute. Bugs stick

Anteaters can lick up to 30,000 termites and ants each day.

to their tongue. Anteaters scrape off bugs with their lower jaw. They swallow whole. They have no teeth. They have a special stomach. Their stomach grinds up the prey.

chapter eight

GIANT SQUIDS

Giant squids are giant. They're 40 feet (12 meters) long. They have a **mantle**. Mantles are the chest area. They have eight arms. They have two feeding **tentacles**. Tentacles are long arms with sucking cups. They snatch prey. They're twice as long as the squid's body.

Giant squids live in the deep ocean. They live in darkness. But they can see in the dark. They have special eyes. They have the largest eyes of any creature. Their eyes are 10 inches (25.4 cm) across. They're the size of large beach balls. They have over a billion receptors. Receptors are like

Colossal squids are bigger than giant squids. They have a longer mantle.

feelers. These feelers line the back of their eyeballs.
They take in more light.

Humboldt squids are jumbo squids. Sometimes, they're confused with Giant Squids.

Giant squids use their eyes to hunt. They track fish. Next, they shoot out their tentacles. They pull in their prey. Then, they use their beak. Their beak crushes food. They use their tongue to eat. Their tongue has small teeth.

Giant squids see far away. Their eyes help them hide from **predators**. A predator is a hunter. Their predator is the sperm whale.

They swim slowly. They have small fins. These fins are at the rear of their mantle. But they use jet **propulsion** to move fast. Propulsion is a push or launch. Their mantle pulls in water. Then, it pushes out water. This lets them get away fast.

WHEN ANIMALS ATTACK!

Female mosquitoes can have deadly bites. They want blood. They have special mouthparts. The mouthparts look like tubes. They're extreme body parts. They're called proboscises. They're long, moving noses. They're like straws. The biting system is special. It's used to suck blood. Female mosquitoes land on skin. They lock in. They dig around. They find blood. They pump out blood. They drink for about 4 minutes. Their spit can cause rashes. It can kill people. Mosquito bites can spread sicknesses. Examples are yellow fever, malaria, and Zika virus. Malaria kills one in 17 people who get it. Zika virus causes fever, red eyes, pain, headaches, and a rash. It affects pregnant women. Pregnant women can give birth to babies with small heads. These babies can have brain problems.

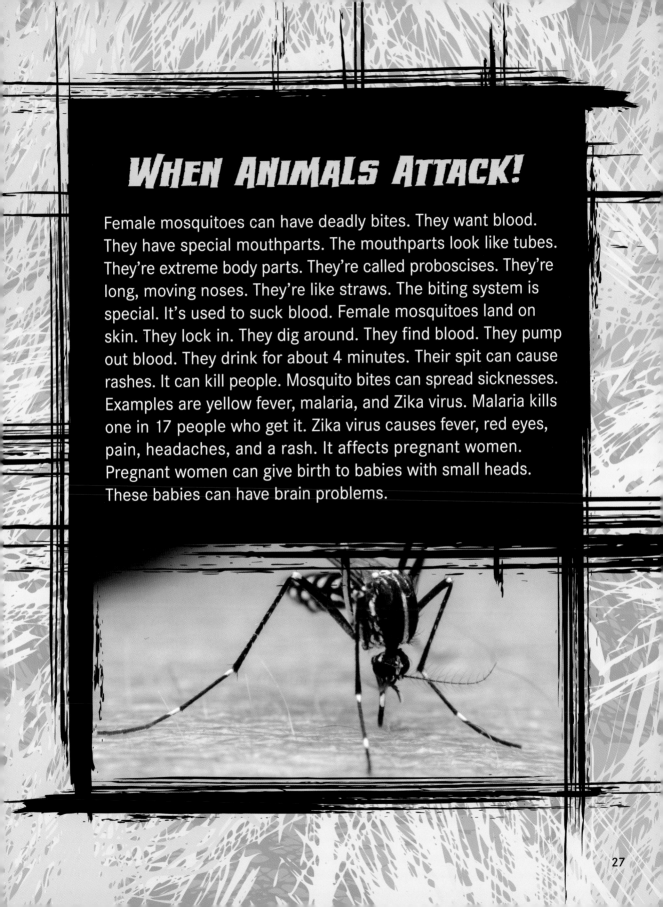

Chapter nine

ELEPHANTS

Elephants live in Africa and Asia. They have a **trunk**. Trunks are a combination of a nose and upper lip.

Trunks have over 100,000 muscles. They're strong. They lift heavy loads. They're **nimble**. Nimble means able to move easily. Trunks have muscles on the tip. The muscles are like a finger. Trunks can do many things. They pick leaves from tall trees. They pluck grass. They drink water. They're used for showering.

Trunks are used to smell. They smell water several miles away. They're used to breathe. Elephants hold their trunks

An elephant's sense of smell is one of the best of any mammal.

above water. They walk across rivers. Trunks are used to make sounds. They are used to touch. Elephants talk to each other. They touch faces. They stroke. They hug.

chapter ten

GIRAFFES

Giraffes live in Africa. They're the world's tallest animals. They're up to 20 feet (6 m) tall. They have tall legs. They have an even longer neck. Giraffes can eat leaves from tall trees. They can see predators.

Their neck is 6 feet (1.8 m) long. Blood has to be pumped up their neck. They have special neck tubes. These tubes control blood flow. This stops giraffes from passing out. It stops deadly head rushes. Giraffes also breathe slowly. They have large lungs. This helps air travel up their neck.

A giraffe's sticky tongue is 20 inches (51 cm) long. Giraffes use it to clean their own ears.

Males use their neck to fight. Their head has two bony horns. They use them to strike other males.

CONSIDER THIS!

TAKE A POSITION! Which animal do you think has the most useless body part? Which animal do you think has the most useful body part? Argue your points with reasons and evidence.

SAY WHAT? Reread this book. Make a T-chart. List the animals' body parts in the left column. List the functions of the body parts in the right column. Write an information paragraph. Explain how animals' body parts help animals survive in their environments.

THINK ABOUT IT! If animals could talk and think like we do, what would they think about human body parts? What do you think they'd find strange about us? List your body parts and explain how each body part helps you survive.

LEARN MORE!

- Jupiter Kids. *Animal Body Parts: Veterinary Anatomy Coloring*. Newark, DE: Speedy Publishing LLC, 2015.
- Loh-Hagan, Virginia. *Top 10: Oddities*. Ann Arbor, MI: 45th Parallel Press, 2016.
- Spelman, Lucy. *Animal Encyclopedia: 2,500 Animals with Photos, Maps, and More!* Washington, DC: National Geographic Children's Books, 2012.

GLOSSARY

bill (BIL) a bird's beak

burrows (BUR-ohz) underground homes or tunnels

canids (KAN-idz) group of animals that include dogs, wolves, and foxes

function (FUHNGK-shuhn) specific job

mammals (MAM-uhlz) animals that have fur or hair, give birth to live young, feed milk to their young, and are warm-blooded

mantle (MAN-tuhl) torso or chest area

mucus (MYOO-kuhs) body snot

nimble (NIM-buhl) able to move easily

nocturnal (nahk-TUR-nuhl) active at night

predators (PRED-uh-turz) hunters

prey (PRAY) animals that are hunted for food

primates (PRYE-mayts) group of animals that includes humans, apes, and monkeys

propulsion (pruh-PUHL-shuhn) launch or push

receptors (rih-SEPT-urz) cells that pick up senses

rodent (ROH-duhnt) small mammal such as a rat or mouse

rotate (ROH-tayt) to turn

tentacles (TEN-tuh-kuhlz) long arms, sometimes with sucking cups

tropical (TRAH-pih-kuhl) hot and wet weather

trunk (TRUHNGK) elephant nose that is a combination of a nose and upper lip

tusks (TUHSKS) long teeth that stick out of the mouth

INDEX